WISE QUOTES: IMMANUEL KANT

(95 IMMANUEL KANT QUOTES)

Vol. 1

Rowan Stevens

A categorical imperative would be one which represented an action as objectively necessary in itself, without reference to any other purpose.

A good will is good not because of what it effects, or accomplishes, not because of its fitness to attain some intended end, but good just by its willing, i.e. in itself; and, considered by itself, it is to be esteemed beyond compare much higher than anything that could ever be brought about by it in favor of some inclinations, and indeed, if you will, the sum of all inclinations. Even if by some particular disfavor of fate, or by the scanty endowment of a stepmotherly nature, this will should entirely lack the capacity to carry through its purpose; if despite its greatest striving it should still accomplish nothing, and only the good will were to remain (not of course, as a mere wish, but as the summoning of all means that are within our control); then, like a jewel, it would still shine by itself, as something that has full worth in itself.

Act in such a way that you treat humanity, whether in your own person or in the person of any other, never merely as a means to an end, but always at the same time as an end.

Act only according to that maxim by which you can at the same time will that it should become a universal law.

All false art, all vain wisdom, lasts its time but finally destroys itself, and its highest culture is also the epoch of its decay.

All human cognition begins with intuitions, proceeds from thence to conceptions, and ends with ideas.

All our knowledge begins with the senses, proceeds then to the understanding, and ends with reason. There is nothing higher than reason.

An action, to have moral worth, must be done from duty.

An age cannot bind itself and ordain to put the succeeding one into such a condition that it cannot extend its (at best very occasional) knowledge, purify itself of errors, and progress in general enlightenment. That would be a crime against human nature, the proper destination of which lies precisely in this progress and the descendants would be fully justified in rejecting those decrees as having been made in an unwarranted and malicious manner.

The touchstone of everything that can be concluded as a law for a people lies in the question whether the people could have imposed such a law on itself.

Anarchy is law and freedom without force.
Despotism is law and force without freedom.
Barbarism force without freedom and law.
Republicanism is force with freedom and law.

As a matter of fact, no other language in the world has received such praise as the Lithuanian language. The garlands of high honour have been taken to Lithuanian people for inventing, elaborating, and introducing the most highly developed human speech with its beautiful and clear phonology. Moreover, according to comparative philology, the Lithuanian language is best qualified to represent the primitive Aryan civilization and culture.

As nature has uncovered from under this hard shell the seed for which she most tenderly cares - the propensity and vocation to free thinking - this gradually works back upon the character of the people, who thereby gradually become capable of managing freedom; finally, it affects the principles of government, which finds it to its advantage to treat men, who are now more than machines, in accordance with their dignity.

Beauty presents an indeterminate concept of Understanding, the sublime an indeterminate concept of Reason.

Better the whole people perish than that injustice be done

But although all our knowledge begins with experience, it does not follow that it arises from experience.

But only he who, himself enlightened, is not afraid of shadows.

But to unite in a permanent religious institution which is not to be subject to doubt before the public even in the lifetime of one man, and thereby to make a period of time fruitless in the progress of mankind toward improvement, thus working to the disadvantage of posterity - that is absolutely forbidden. For himself (and only for a short time) a man may postpone enlightenment in what he ought to know, but to renounce it for posterity is to injure and trample on the rights of mankind.

But, above all, it will confer an inestimable benefit on morality and religion, by showing that all the objections urged against them may be silenced forever by the Socratic method, that is to say, by proving the ignorance of the objector.

By a lie a man throws away and as it were annihilates his dignity as a man

Coffee! Coffee!

!

Dare to know! Have the courage to use your own intelligence!

Dare to think!

Deficiency in judgement is properly that which is called stupidity; and for such a failing we know no remedy. A dull or narrow-minded person, to whom nothing is wanting but a proper degree of understanding, may be improved by tuition, even so far as to deserve the epithet of learned. But as such persons frequently labour under a deficiency in the faculty of judgement, it is not uncommon to find men extremely learned who in the application of their science betray a lamentable degree this irremediable want.

Dignity is a value that creates irreplaceability.

Enlightenment is man's release from his self-incurred tutelage. Tutelage is man's inability to make use of his understanding without direction from another. Self-incurred is this tutelage when its cause lies not in lack of reason but in lack of resolution and courage to use it without direction from another. Sapere aude! 'Have courage to use your own reason!'- that is the motto of enlightenment.

Experience without theory is blind, but theory without experience is mere intellectual play.

For peace to reign on Earth, humans must evolve into new beings who have learned to see the whole first.

From such crooked wood as that which man is made of, nothing straight can be fashioned.

Genius is the ability to independently arrive at and understand concepts that would normally have to be taught by another person.

Give me matter and I will build a world out of it.

Have patience awhile; slanders are not long-lived. Truth is the child of time; erelong she shall appear to vindicate thee.

Have the courage to use your own reason- That is the motto of enlightenment.

He who is cruel to animals becomes hard also in his dealings with men. We can judge the heart of a man by his treatment of animals.

He who would know the world must first manufacture it.

High towers, and metaphysically-great men resembling them, round both of which there is commonly much wind, are not for me. My place is the fruitful bathos, the bottom-land, of experience; and the word transcendental, does not signify something passing beyond all experience, but something that indeed precedes it a priori, but that is intended simply to make cognition of experience possible.

How then is perfection to be sought? Wherein lies our hope? In education, and in nothing else.

Human beings are never to be treated as a means but always as ends.

Human reason, in one sphere of its cognition, is called upon to consider questions, which it cannot decline, as they are presented by its own nature, but which it cannot answer, as they transcend every faculty of the mind.

I had to deny knowledge in order to make room for faith.

If adversity and hopeless grief have quite taken away the taste for life; if an unfortunate man, strong of soul and more indignant about his fate than despondent or dejected, wishes for death and yet preserves his life without loving it, not from inclination or fear but from duty, then his maxim has moral content.

If I have a book that thinks for me, a pastor who acts as my conscience, a physician who prescribes my diet, and so on... then I have no need to exert myself. I have no need to think, if only I can pay; others will take care of that disagreeable business for me.

If the truth shall kill them, let them die.

In all judgements by which we describe anything as beautiful, we allow no one to be of another opinion.

In every department of physical science there is only so much science, properly so-called, as there is mathematics.

In the kingdom of ends everything has either a price or a dignity. What has a price can be replaced by something else as its equivalent; what on the other hand is raised above all price and therefore admits of no equivalent has a dignity.

Innocence is a splendid thing, only it has the misfortune not to keep very well and to be easily misled.

It is beyond a doubt that all our knowledge begins with experience.

It is of great consequence to have previously determined the concept that one wants to elucidate through observation before questioning experience about it; for one finds in experience what one needs only if one knows in advance what to look for.

It is the Land of Truth (enchanted name!), surrounded by a wide and stormy ocean, the true home of illusion, where many a fog bank and ice, that soon melts away, tempt us to believe in new lands, while constantly deceiving the adventurous mariner with vain hopes, and involving him in adventures which he can never leave, yet never bring to an end.

It was the duty of philosophy to destroy the illusions which had their origin in misconceptions, whatever darling hopes and valued expectations may be ruined by its explanations.

Laughter is an affect resulting from the sudden transformation of a heightened expectation into nothing.

Laziness and cowardice are the reasons why so great a portion of mankind, after nature has long since discharged them from external direction (naturaliter maiorennes), nevertheless remains under lifelong tutelage, and why it is so easy for others to set themselves up as their guardians. It is so easy not to be of age. If I have a book which understands for me, a pastor who has a conscience for me, a physician who decides my diet, and so forth, I need not trouble myself. I need not think, if I can only pay - others will easily undertake the irksome work for me.

That the step to competence is held to be very dangerous by the far greater portion of mankind...

Lithuanian nation must be saved, as it is the key to all the riddles - not only philology, but also in history - to solve the puzzle.

Look closely. The beautiful may be small.

Man must be disciplined, for he is by nature raw and wild.

Man, and in general every rational being, exists as an end in himself, not merely as a means for arbitrary use by this or that will: he must in all his actions, whether they are directed to himself or to other rational beings, always be viewed at the same time as an end.

Marriage...is the union of two people of different sexes with a view to the mutual possession of each other's sexual attributes for the duration of their lives.

Mathematics, natural science, laws, arts, even morality, etc. do not completely fill the soul; there is always a space left over reserved for pure and speculative reason, the emptiness of which prompts us to seek in vagaries, buffooneries, and mysticism for what seems to be employment and entertainment, but what actually is mere pastime undertaken in order to deaden the troublesome voice of reason, which, in accordance with its nature, requires something that can satisfy it and does not merely subserve other ends or the interests of our inclinations.

Metaphysics... is nothing but the inventory of all we possess through pure reason, ordered systematically. Nothing here can escape us, because what reason brings forth entirely out of itself cannot be hidden, but is brought to light by reason itself as soon as reason's common principle has been discovered. The perfect unity of this kind of cognition, and the fact that it arises solely out of pure concepts without any influence that would extend or increase it from experience or even particular intuition, which would lead to a determinate experience, make this unconditioned completeness not only feasible but also necessary. Tecum habita, et noris quam sit tibi curta supellex. Dwell in your own house, and you will know how simple your possessions are.

Morality is not properly the doctrine of how we may make ourselves happy, but how we may make ourselves worthy of happiness.

Nature is beautiful because it looks like Art; and Art can only be called beautiful if we are conscious of it as Art while yet it looks like Nature.

New prejudices will serve as well as old ones to harness the great unthinking masses.

For this enlightenment, however, nothing is required but freedom, and indeed the most harmless among all the things to which this term can properly be applied. It is the freedom to make public use of one's reason at every point. But I hear on all sides, 'Do not argue!' The Officer says: 'Do not argue but drill!' The tax collector: 'Do not argue but pay!' The cleric: 'Do not argue but believe!' Only one prince in the world says, 'Argue as much as you will, and about what you will, but obey!' Everywhere there is restriction on freedom.

Nothing can possibly be conceived in the world, or even out of it, which can be called good, without qualification, except a good will.

Nothing is divine but what is agreeable to reason.

One who makes himself a worm cannot complain afterwards if people step on him.

Only the descent into the hell of self-knowledge can pave the way to godliness.

Our age is the age of criticism, to which everything must be subjected. The sacredness of religion, and the authority of legislation, are by many regarded as grounds of exemption from the examination of this tribunal. But, if they on they are exempted, they become the subjects of just suspicion, and cannot lay claim to sincere respect, which reason accords only to that which has stood the test of a free and public examination.

Out of the crooked timber of humanity, no straight thing was even made.

Rules for happiness: something to do, someone to love, something to hope for.

Sapere aude.

Seek not the favor of the multitude; it is seldom got by honest and lawful means. But seek the testimony of few; and number not voices, but weigh them.

Settle, for sure and universally, what conduct will promote the happiness of a rational being.

Simply to acquiesce in skepticism can never suffice to overcome the restlessness of reason.

Skepticism is thus a resting-place for human reason, where it can reflect upon its dogmatic wanderings and make survey of the region in which it finds itself, so that for the future it may be able to choose its path with more certainty. But it is no dwelling-place for permanent settlement. Such can be obtained only through perfect certainty in our knowledge, alike of the objects themselves and of the limits within which all our knowledge of objects is enclosed.

Space and time are the framework within which the mind is constrained to construct its experience of reality.

Standing armies constantly threaten other nations with war by giving the appearance that they are prepared for it, which goads nations into competing with one another in the number of men under arms, and this practice knows no bounds. And since the costs related to maintaining peace will in this way finally become greater than those of a short war, standing armies are the cause of wars of aggression that are intended to end burdensome expenditures. Moreover, paying men to kill or be killed appears to use them as mere machines and tools in the hands of another (the nation), which is inconsistent with the rights of humanity.

The busier we are, the more acutely we feel that we live, the more conscious we are of life.

The death of dogma is the birth of morality.

The light dove, in free flight cutting through the air the resistance of which it feels, could get the idea that it could do even better in airless space. Likewise, Plato abandoned the world of the senses because it posed so many hindrances for the understanding, and dared to go beyond it on the wings of the ideas, in the empty space of pure understanding.

The people naturally adhere most to doctrines which demand the least self-exertion and the least use of their own reason, and which can best accommodate their duties to their inclinations.

The reading of all good books is like a conversation with the finest minds of past centuries.

The schematicism by which our understanding deals with the phenomenal world ... is a skill so deeply hidden in the human soul that we shall hardly guess the secret trick that Nature here employs.

The whole interest of my reason, whether speculative or practical, is concentrated in the three following questions: What can I know? What should I do? What may I hope?

There is something splendid about innocence; but what is bad about it, in turn, is that it cannot protect itself very well and is easily seduced.

Thoughts without content are empty, intuitions without concepts are blind. The understanding can intuit nothing, the senses can think nothing. Only through their unison can knowledge arise.

!

To be is to do.

Treat people as an end, and never as a means to an end.

Two things fill the mind with ever new and increasing admiration and awe, the more often and steadily we reflect upon them: the starry heavens above me and the moral law within me. I do not seek or conjecture either of them as if they were veiled obscurities or extravagances beyond the horizon of my vision; I see them before me and connect them immediately with the consciousness of my existence.

War seems to be ingrained in human nature, and even to be regarded as something noble to which man is inspired by his love of honor, without selfish motives.

We are enriched not by what we possess, but by what we can do without.

What might be said of things in themselves, separated from all relationship to our senses, remains for us absolutely unknown

When he puts a thing on a pedestal and calls it beautiful, he demands the same delight from others. He judges not merely for himself, but for all men, and then speaks of beauty as if it were the property of things.

When the tremulous radiance of a summer night fills with twinkling stars and the moon itself is full, I am slowly drawn into a state of enhanced sensitivity made of friendship and disdain for the world and eternity.

Whereas the beautiful is limited, the sublime is limitless, so that the mind in the presence of the sublime, attempting to imagine what it cannot, has pain in the failure but pleasure in contemplating the immensity of the attempt

Without man and his potential for moral progress, the whole of reality would be a mere wilderness, a thing in vain, and have no final purpose.

Woman wants control, man self-control.

www.ingramcontent.com/pod-product-compliance
Lightning Source LLC
Chambersburg PA
CBHW071256070526
44583CB00017B/2499